# 30 Day Virtual Book Tour Challenge *for Authors*

## Take Your Book on Tour Around the Globe Without Leaving Home!

## D'vorah Lansky, M.Ed.

Vibrant Marketing Publications
Hartford, CT

Published by Vibrant Marketing Publications
Copyright ©2016 D'vorah Lansky

www.ActionGuidesForAuthors.com

ISBN 978-0-9967431-8-1

# Dedication

This book is dedicated to the amazing authors in our
Virtual Book Tour programs!
Your enthusiasm and dedication to sharing your
book and your message with the world is inspiring!

Here's to your continued
virtual book tour success!

# Table of Contents

# Table of Contents

# Introduction

A virtual book tour is much like a traditional book tour, but instead of authors traveling from city to city and venue to venue, hoping there will be a crowd when they arrive, they travel virtually, to a variety of targeted blogs and podcasts across the Internet.

During your virtual book tour, you have the opportunity to be hosted by people in your industry who will help to promote you and introduce you to their audiences. In this way, you'll gain credibility and your book will be exposed to many new audiences As you travel from blog to blog and podcast to podcast, you share your message in the form of audio author interviews or as written articles, known as blog posts.

It takes time to put all the pieces of a virtual book tour in place. By planning ahead and segmenting your projects, you can accomplish a great deal. You can pull together a virtual book tour in as little as eight weeks. However, it's advisable to begin planning at least three months in advance. That way you'll have plenty of time to:

- Identify your target audience
- Set up or update your blog
- Build relationships with potential hosts
- Line up tour hosts
- Prepare content
- Promote your tour
- Interact with readers

A virtual tour provides you with exposure for your book, now and into the future. By mapping out your schedule and segmenting your activities, you'll efficiently accomplish a great deal, have the opportunity to interact with readers, and enjoy your virtual book tour journey.

# How to Use This Action Guide

In this action guide you'll find bite-size action steps that will allow you to develop your virtual book tour one step at a time. To make the most of this opportunity, open up your calendar and schedule at least three time slots per week, for 4-6 weeks, to go through this action guide and apply what you learn. Before you know it you'll be taking your book on tour, on the virtual book tour road!

# Notes

# Step One

## *Set the Stage for Your Virtual Book Tour*

Activities 1-4

As you prepare to take your book on a virtual book tour, it's essential that you get clear on your goals, that you identify who your niche audience is, and that you take steps towards scheduling your tour dates.

In this module you'll have the opportunity to participate in activities that will help you to gain clarity and focus in these areas.

Activity #1                    Date: _____

# Get Clear on Your Virtual Book Tour Goals

Today's action step is to get clear on your "why" for wanting to participate in a virtual book tour. You'll also have the opportunity to give thought to how your readers can benefit by having access to you and your book or business.

Getting clear on your "why" will provide you with motivation and inspiration for putting together a virtual book tour, where you'll connect with your niche audience and leaders in your field. What is your "why" for wanting to participate in a virtual book tour? Turn to the facing page and complete the suggested activities. Getting clear on your "why" will fuel your passion for participating in a virtual book tour.

At the end of the day, journal your accomplishments in the section provided below. By prioritizing time to take action and reflect on your activity and results each day, you'll maximize the benefits you'll receive from this opportunity.

## What I Accomplished Today

# Action Steps

## What is Your "Why" for Producing a Virtual Book Tour

What is your "why" for wanting to participate in a virtual book tour?_____

_____

_____

_____

What is your "why" for wanting to reach more readers? _____

_____

_____

_____

How will your target audience benefit by having access to your tour? _____

_____

_____

_____

How will you benefit by gaining more exposure in your niche? _____

_____

_____

_____

# Activity #2

## Identify Your Niche Audience

Today's action step is to identify your niche audience. By knowing who your ideal readers are, you'll be able to develop relationships with those who want and need what you have to offer. This creates a win/win situation.

Turn to the facing page and spend some time identifying who your target audience is. This is essential as it will allow you to maximize your efforts and your results while helping the exact people who need what you have to offer. Once you've identified your niche audience, it will be easy for you to identify and locate blog owners and podcast hosts who serve this audience.

At the end of the day, journal your accomplishments in the section provided below. By prioritizing time to take action and reflect on your activity and results each day, you'll maximize the benefits you'll receive from this opportunity.

## What I Accomplished Today

# Action Steps

## Identify Your Target Audience

Knowing who your ideal readers are will serve you well as you plan for your virtual book tour. Throughout your tour, you'll focus on gaining exposure to this audience.

Describe your ideal student, client, or reader: _____

_____

_____

_____


What are they most interested in?

○ _____

○ _____

○ _____


What are the top three things they struggle with?

○ _____

○ _____

○ _____


What do they want most in life?

○ _____

○ _____

○ _____

Activity #3                    Date: _____

# Decide on the Dates for Your Tour

Today's action step is to decide on your virtual book tour dates. For a first tour, I recommend 9-12 days. These can be consecutive days or on Mondays, Wednesdays, and Fridays for three or four weeks, for example.

How many tour stops would you like to have for your virtual book tour: _____

Open up your calendar a month or two in the future, and plug in the dates for your virtual book tour. You can always adjust the dates, however having dates in your calendar will make it real and will allow you to schedule hosts.

The firm or tentative dates for my tour are: _____

The days of the week I'll be touring are: _____

At the end of the day, journal your accomplishments in the section provided below. By prioritizing time to take action and reflect on your activity and results each day, you'll maximize the benefits you'll receive from this opportunity.

## What I Accomplished Today

# Monthly Calendar for: Month:_____ Year:_____

(Decide when you'll conduct your tour. Fill in the dates & line up tour stops.)

| Monday | Tuesday | Wednesday | Thursday | Friday |
|--------|---------|-----------|----------|--------|
|        |         |           |          |        |
|        |         |           |          |        |
|        |         |           |          |        |
|        |         |           |          |        |
|        |         |           |          |        |
|        |         |           |          |        |

# Monthly Calendar for: Month:_____ Year:_____

(Decide when you'll conduct your tour. Fill in the dates & line up tour stops.)

| Monday | Tuesday | Wednesday | Thursday | Friday |
|--------|---------|-----------|----------|--------|
|        |         |           |          |        |
|        |         |           |          |        |
|        |         |           |          |        |
|        |         |           |          |        |
|        |         |           |          | 15     |

Activity #4                    Date: _____

# Reach Out and Line Up a Few Tour Hosts

Today's action step is to make a list of three people you know, who attract your target audience and ask them to be hosts for your virtual book tour. By beginning with people you know, you'll get the ball rolling and you'll pave the way to getting your virtual book tour booked.

Begin by making a list of people you personally know, who your ideal reader would be interested in. If your readers are interested in their topic, then their readers will be interested in your topic. By having a few hosts lined up, before you begin reaching out to people you don't yet know, it will give your virtual book tour more credibility and create interest.

At the end of the day, journal your accomplishments in the section provided below. By prioritizing time to take action and reflect on your activity and results each day, you'll maximize the benefits you'll receive from this opportunity.

## What I Accomplished Today

# Action Steps

## Line Up Your First Few Virtual Book Tour Hosts

The easiest way to get the ball rolling is to reach out to a few people you know, who write or speak on topics of interest to your niche audience, and get them lined up as tour hosts for your virtual book tour.

Make a list of three people you know, who have a blog or podcast that would be of interest to your niche audience. Reach out to them and invite them to host you.

- ☐ _____
- ☐ _____
- ☐ _____

Create a Virtual Book Tour Schedule Page on your blog. When potential hosts see this page and recognize their colleagues, it will be easy for them to say "yes!" As you line up hosts, add them to this schedule page. List their name and the name of their blog or podcast. You can also add a photograph of each host, which will make it very easy for visitors and potential hosts to recognize known people in your industry.

Ask each person who says "yes" for a referral to a potential host in your niche.

- ☐ _____
- ☐ _____
- ☐ _____

**Sample Email:** Hi [name], I've been thinking of you and would love to hear what's going on in your world. I'd like to share my update and invite you to be featured in my upcoming virtual book tour. The book I'll be featuring on my tour is [name of book.]

Here's the scoop... I've decided to take my book on a virtual book tour, where I'll be traveling to blogs and podcasts that attract our mutual ideal reader. I'd love to feature your [blog/podcast] as a destination site for this event. The virtual book tour will generate a lot of exposure to audiences who are interested in your topic.

As a host, you'd feature a blog post on your blog, provided by me, on a topic our readers would benefit from. Alternatively, we could record an interview.

You are of course under no obligation so please take a moment to reply and let me know whether or not you'd like me to reserve one of the featured tour stops for you. Thank you! With warmest regards, [Name]

# Notes

# Potential Hosts Tracking Sheet

| Name | Date Contacted | Blog or Podcast | Name of Show or Site | Yes/No | Tour Date |
|------|----------------|-----------------|----------------------|--------|-----------|
|      |                |                 |                      |        |           |
|      |                |                 |                      |        |           |
|      |                |                 |                      |        |           |
|      |                |                 |                      |        |           |
|      |                |                 |                      |        |           |
|      |                |                 |                      |        |           |
|      |                |                 |                      |        |           |
|      |                |                 |                      |        |           |
|      |                |                 |                      |        |           |
|      |                |                 |                      |        |           |
|      |                |                 |                      |        |           |
|      |                |                 |                      |        |           |
|      |                |                 |                      |        |           |
|      |                |                 |                      |        |           |
|      |                |                 |                      |        |           |

# Referrals from the Above Hosts

| Name | Date Contacted | Blog or Podcast | Name of Show or Site | Yes/No | Tour Date |
|------|----------------|-----------------|----------------------|--------|-----------|
|      |                |                 |                      |        |           |
|      |                |                 |                      |        |           |
|      |                |                 |                      |        |           |
|      |                |                 |                      |        |           |
|      |                |                 |                      |        |           |
|      |                |                 |                      |        |           |
|      |                |                 |                      |        |           |
|      |                |                 |                      |        |           |
|      |                |                 |                      |        |           |
|      |                |                 |                      |        |           |
|      |                |                 |                      |        |           |
|      |                |                 |                      |        |           |
|      |                |                 |                      |        |           |
|      |                |                 |                      |        |           |
|      |                |                 |                      |        |           |

# My Master Tour Schedule

## Add Confirmed Tour Stops as You Schedule Them

☐ Date of Tour Stop: _____ Host:_____

Tour Stop URL: _____

Notes: _____

☐ Date of Tour Stop: _____ Host:_____

Tour Stop URL: _____

Notes: _____

☐ Date of Tour Stop: _____ Host:_____

Tour Stop URL: _____

Notes: _____

☐ Date of Tour Stop: _____ Host:_____

Tour Stop URL: _____

Notes: _____

☐ Date of Tour Stop: _____ Host:_____

Tour Stop URL: _____

Notes: _____

☐ Date of Tour Stop: _____ Host:_____

Tour Stop URL: _____

Notes: _____

# My Master Tour Schedule
### Add Confirmed Tour Stops as You Schedule Them

☐ Date of Tour Stop: _____    Host:_____

Tour Stop URL: _____

Notes: _____

☐ Date of Tour Stop: _____    Host:_____

Tour Stop URL: _____

Notes: _____

☐ Date of Tour Stop: _____    Host:_____

Tour Stop URL: _____

Notes: _____

☐ Date of Tour Stop: _____    Host:_____

Tour Stop URL: _____

Notes: _____

☐ Date of Tour Stop: _____    Host:_____

Tour Stop URL: _____

Notes: _____

☐ Date of Tour Stop: _____    Host:_____

Tour Stop URL: _____

Notes: _____

# Notes

_____     _____

_____     _____

_____     _____

_____     _____

_____     _____

_____     _____

_____     _____

_____     _____

_____     _____

_____     _____

_____     _____

_____     _____

# Step Two
## *Develop Your Author Platform*

Activities
5-8

Your author platform can be compared to a "stage." It lifts you up and allows you to become more visible. Your online author platform includes things such as; your author blog, your social media presence, your Amazon presence, and more.

In this module we focus on enhancing your online author platform so you are able to reach more readers, gain credibility, and sell more books.

Activity #5                Date: _____

# Get Your Blog Ready for Company

Today's action step is to streamline your blog. Your blog can become the center of your online world. It's the place that people come to connect with you, find out more about your work, and even buy your book. Having a blog provides you with a platform for sharing your ideas and a place where you can connect with your readers.

Your blog can focus on your message, your book, and/or you as an author. If you already have a blog, you'll want to tidy things up and prepare for company. If you do not yet have a blog, you may want to set one up or hire someone to set your blog up for you.

At the end of the day, journal your accomplishments in the section provided below. By prioritizing time to take action and reflect on your activity and results each day, you'll maximize the benefits you'll receive from this opportunity.

## What I Accomplished Today

# Action Steps

## Streamline Your Blog & Get Ready for Company

Before you begin your virtual book tour, you'll want to update and streamline your blog. For many people today, their blog also functions as their website. If you do not yet have a blog, you may want to set one up or hire someone to set your blog up for you.

You may already have an established blog. If you do, head over and view it from the eyes of your readers. Be sure that your site is attractive and welcoming and it is clear as to what the focus of your site is.

Take time to go through your site and make sure to:

- ☐ Test all links to make sure they are leading to where you want them to go.
- ☐ That all links taking people off of your site open in a new page. That way the window to your blog will remain open in their browser.
- ☐ Clean up posts, pages, and images.
- ☐ Make sure that all of the content on your site is current and relevant.
- ☐ Add key pages to your blog and add content to each of these pages.

Here are examples of some of the key pages you may want to have as part of your blog. Refer to the suggestions on the following pages as you prepare your blog for your virtual book tour.

- ☐ About Page
- ☐ Endorsements or Reviews Page
- ☐ Media Page
- ☐ Events Page (or Virtual Book Tour Page)
- ☐ Blog Page
- ☐ Contact or Support Page

**The About Page** is a place where people can find out more about you and your book or programs. The first thing you'll want to have is a professional headshot photograph, with you smiling. This will provide a warm welcome to your visitors and help them to feel a connection with you.

Next, share a brief paragraph or two about you that provides a rich introduction, highlighting your experience and your expertise. You may also want to include links to your profile on up to three social networks. You can include information about your book on your about page, or you may want to create a separate page about your book.

**The Endorsements Page** tells people more about you and your book. This is where you can feature the endorsements, reviews, or testimonials, from experts in your field as well as from your colleagues and readers. These can be endorsements that you've included on the cover and/or inside of your book as well as new ones that are posted on Amazon or that you gather over time. Be sure to add the photograph of the person giving the endorsement as this lends more credibility to their contribution.

**The Blog Page** is where the blog posts show up. Typically, each time you publish a new post, the newest post will show up at the top of the page. We call this "dynamic" content, as it is always changing, while your other pages provide static content, which changes only when you go in to that page to change the content. On the blog page, the content changes each time you add a new blog post.

When composing a blog post, you have the opportunity to add that post to a specific category. Typically, the default setting is to have all of your blog posts appear on the blog page. You do however have the option of having only posts in a specific category appear on your blog page. You'll need to explore your blog's theme settings to make this adjustment.

**The Events Page** is where you provide a list of live and virtual events, past, present, and future. Having a "schedule of events" section provides an easy way for your audience to connect with you and learn more about you and your book. Your Events page can include details about upcoming in-person events, such as book signings, as well as virtual events, such as your virtual book tour. Make sure to include easy-to-access details to encourage audience participation.

You can also set up a Virtual Book Tour page, in addition to or instead of an Events Page. On your virtual book tour page, you can include your tour schedule and links to each of your tour stops.

**The Media Page** is where you share your activity, articles, press releases, photos, book cover images, author bio, speaking engagements, etc. Your media page can also provide links to previous interviews, blog posts, newspaper and magazine articles and more.

On your media page, you can also provide a one page PDF document, such as a Speaker One Sheet, for potential interview hosts. To do this create a Word document and include your 100-150 word author bio, photograph, book cover image, and a proposed list of interview questions. Save it as a PDF file and upload it to your media page. If you have not participated in many interviews or done much guest blogging, be creative as you pull your initial media page content together. Draw from the above and know that you can always make changes as you have more information to add.

**The Contact Page** provides you with a way to be reached by your audience. You can add your contact information here or you can add a contact form which people can fill in and submit. A contact form makes it easy for people to submit their question or request, while providing you with the opportunity to respond at a time that is good for you.

Activity #6          Date: _____

# Enhance Your Amazon Author Page

Today's action step is to set up and/or enhance your Amazon Author Page.

One of the most powerful "secret weapons" for an author is Amazon's Author Central page. Each author, with a published (print or Kindle) book, can set up their own page, which includes a myriad of marketing tools.

Enhancing your Amazon Author page can increase your book sales, as you'll have a more professional looking presence on Amazon.

At the end of the day, journal your accomplishments in the section provided below. By prioritizing time to take action and reflect on your activity and results each day, you'll maximize the benefits you'll receive from this opportunity.

## What I Accomplished Today

# Action Steps

## Enhance Your Amazon Author Page

Amazon Author Central is a free service that allows authors to create an author page on Amazon. If you're an author with a print or Kindle book listed in the Amazon catalog, you are eligible to join Amazon Author Central.

If you don't have a published book, you may want to write and publish even a brief, 3,000-7,000 word Kindle book. This will allow you to set up your Amazon Author Page. Brief Kindle books can be "top tips" or "7 ways" types of books, for example. They can also be brief books on a subject related to your topic area.

Here are seven ways that you can enhance your Amazon Author Page:

- ○ Register for an Amazon Author Central Account
- ○ Add a brief yet informative biography
- ○ Upload your author photo
- ○ Claim your vanity URL
- ○ Add your blog feed
- ○ Make sure your bibliography is up to date
- ○ Upload a video or video book trailer

Turn the page for detailed instructions for accomplishing the above. Once your Amazon Author Page has been updated, you can share it with the world!

# 7 Ways to Enhance Your Amazon Author Central Page

## Step 1: Register for an Amazon Author Central Account

Go to Amazon Author Central to register at authorcentral.amazon.com. You can login with the same email and password as your Amazon Customer account. Note: you must have a print or Kindle book published on Amazon in order register for an Amazon Author Central page. If your book has not yet been published, you can still go through this lesson in preparation of having a published book.

## Step 2: Include a Brief, Yet Informative, Biography

The next thing you'll want to do is add a brief, yet informative biography. Share your credentials and accomplishments as well as a bit about "what you do," as it relates to you as an author. Write your biography in the third person as it sounds more professional and gives you more credibility.

## Step 3: Upload Your Author Photo

The next step is to add a professional, headshot photo to your profile. Make sure that you are smiling and you look friendly and approachable. This is the first thing visitors will see when they come to your page.

You can also upload other photographs, such as photos of your book. Take note though, as you add images, they will move to the #1 spot in your image gallery. The image in the #1 spot is the one that will show up on your profile. That's not a problem though as you can easily click to edit your photos and move them around to change the order.

## Step 4: Claim Your Vanity URL

Another feature on the Author Central page is the ability to add a vanity URL. This will make it really easy for you to direct people to your profile. To set up your vanity URL, login to your profile dashboard and head to the top right of the page. You'll see text inviting you to set up your custom URL. Be sure to choose carefully as you may not be able to change it once you've created it. As an example, here's what mine looks like: Amazon.com/author/dvorahlansky.

## Step 5: Add Your Blog Feed

Adding your blog feed is another way to create a connection with your profile visitors while demonstrating your expertise on a topic. This will help you to build relationships with your readers as well as sell more books. It's easy to pull in titles and excerpts of blog posts from your site by adding your feed URL to the appropriate place on your profile dashboard. Typically your blog feed would be formatted like this: http://YourWebAddress.com/feed

## Step 6: Make Sure All Your Books Are Showing Up in Your Bibliography

If you have published more than one book, you'll want to make sure that they show up on the bibliography section of your Author Central page. If you find that books are missing, you can simply login to the dashboard of your profile and click on the "books" tab. Be sure to add the books you've written as well as ones where you are a contributing author.

## Step 7: Upload a Video or Book Trailer

You can easily upload videos to your Author Central profile. You can share a video book trailer, video tips or excerpts from your book, as examples. One of the easiest way to create videos is by creating PowerPoint slides and recording your slide show along with audio narration.

You can either do this right inside of PowerPoint, or with screen capture programs such as JingProject (JingProject.com) or Camtasia (CamtasiaStudio.com.) Another fun way to create a video is with a program called Animoto (Animoto.com.) You can easily create very professional looking videos.

Activity #7          Date: _____

# **Streamline Your Social Media Profiles**

Today's action step is to streamline your social media profiles. (Facebook, LinkedIn, Pinterest, etc.) Check to make sure you are using the same headshot photograph on each network. This will expand your brand and allow you to become familiar to your audience.

You'll also want to update your biography to ensure that your information is current. Turn to the worksheet on the following page and identify your top three favorite social networks. Participate in the suggested activities as you update your profile and create a cohesive branded social media presence.

At the end of the day, journal your accomplishments in the section provided below. By prioritizing time to take action and reflect on your activity and results each day, you'll maximize the benefits you'll receive from this opportunity.

## What I Accomplished Today

# Action Steps

## Identify 3 Key Social Networks and Streamline Your Profiles

**Name of Social Network:** _____

What I Like Most About This Social Network: _____

My Favorite Groups or Forums on this Site: _____

_____    _____

☐ Use the same photograph that you're using on all social networks

☐ Update your biography and add links to your blog and social networks.

☐ Schedule time, at least once a week, to spend on this site

**Name of Social Network:** _____

What I Like Most About This Social Network: _____

My Favorite Groups or Forums on this Site: _____

_____    _____

☐ Use the same photograph that you're using on all social networks

☐ Update your biography and add links to your blog and social networks.

☐ Schedule time, at least once a week, to spend on this site

**Name of Social Network:** _____

What I Like Most About This Social Network: _____

My Favorite Groups or Forums on this Site: _____

_____    _____

☐ Use the same photograph that you're using on all social networks

☐ Update your biography and add links to your blog and social networks.

☐ Schedule time, at least once a week, to spend on this site

# Create Your Facebook Book or Author Page

Today's action step is to set up your Facebook Book or Author Page. Facebook is currently considered to be the top social network in the world. Having a presence on Facebook is important for an author, as it gives you more exposure and provides an effective way for your audience to connect with you.

Having a Facebook author page provides you with opportunities to share your work and your book, as well as connect with people interested in your topic. A Facebook page can serve as an online community center where your readers come to find out more about your book and where they can interact with you.

At the end of the day, journal your accomplishments in the section provided below. By prioritizing time to take action and reflect on your activity and results each day, you'll maximize the benefits you'll receive from this opportunity.

## What I Accomplished Today

# Action Steps

## Set Up Your Facebook Book or Author Page

Having a Facebook page provides an easy way for you to: answer questions, announce and promote events, and interact with your audience.

- ☐ Login to your Facebook account. Currently you can create a page by clicking on the "home" tab at the top of the page, then on the "pages" tab to the left of the page, and then on the "create a page button" at the top right of the page.
- ☐ From there, you'll be given a choice of categories. The "Author" category falls under the "Artist, Band, or Public Figure" tab.
- ☐ As you set up your page, give strategic thought to what you want to call your page. As an author, using your name—or your name followed by the word "author"—provides you with a branding opportunity.
- ☐ You can further brand your author page by adding your photograph and uploading images related to your topic and book.

Once you've published your Facebook page, it's time to add content.

- ☐ Fill in the "about" section of your page to let visitors know what the focus of your page is
- ☐ Upload your photo or logo
- ☐ Create and upload your Facebook cover (header) image
- ☐ Post a welcome message
- ☐ Schedule time in your calendar to post to your Facebook page, at least once a week. (Daily during your virtual book tour.)

Once you have your branded author page set up, it's time to invite people to "like" your page and join in the conversation.

- ☐ Post a welcoming message and invite people to introduce themselves.
- ☐ You can also add conversation starters, polls, and questions
- ☐ Before too long, people will be interacting with one another and starting new conversations.

# Notes

# Step Three
# *Build Ongoing Relationships with Your Readers*

Your email list is the foundation of a successful online business. During your virtual book tour you'll have opportunities to invite readers and listeners to subscribe to your list, in exchange for a downloadable gift. This will allow you to grow an ongoing relationship with your readers.

Activity #9                    Date: _____

# Create a Downloadable Subscriber Opt-in Gift

Today's action step is to create a downloadable opt-in gift. As part of your virtual book tour, people will visit your blog. An effective way to grow your business and relationships with your blog visitors is to have a way for them to subscribe to your email list via an opt-in form on your site.

You can offer your readers a special report, a chapter of your book, or access to other content, in PDF format, in exchange for their name and email address. By subscribing to your list, people are giving you permission to communicate with them and this will provide you with opportunities to develop an ongoing relationship with your subscribers.

At the end of the day, journal your accomplishments in the section provided below. By prioritizing time to take action and reflect on your activity and results each day, you'll maximize the benefits you'll receive from this opportunity.

## What I Accomplished Today

# Action Steps

## Create a Downloadable Opt-in Gift

The easiest way to create a downloadable opt-in gift for your audience is to compose your content in a Word document and then save it to PDF format.

You want your opt-in gift to be on a subject that is of great interest to your niche audience. People love checklists, top tips lists, and how-tos.

Here are some great idea joggers for an opt-in gift:

- ○ Five Top Tops to…

- ○ 7 Ways to …

- ○ Fast Easy Recipes You Can Make in Fifteen Minutes

- ○ Take Action Checklists to Help You...

- ○ A PDF file is the easiest file format for your gift.


In the space below, jot down your ideas for a gift you could create:

_____

_____

_____

_____

_____

## Add an Opt-In Form to Your Blog

Today's action step is to add an opt-in form to your blog. An opt-in form is where your readers can enter their name and email address in exchange for a downloadable gift. You'll need to register for an email service, such as AWeber, in order to do this. These companies usually offer tutorials and great customer support.

Your email service will provide you with the code needed to create your opt-in form. Typically, you'll find a wide variety of opt-in form designs to choose from. This will allow you to carry your branded colors through to your opt-in form.

At the end of the day, journal your accomplishments in the section provided below. By prioritizing time to take action and reflect on your activity and results each day, you'll maximize the benefits you'll receive from this opportunity.

### What I Accomplished Today

# Action Steps

## Add an Opt-In Form to Your Blog

Growing your email list will allow you to develop an ongoing relationship with your subscribers. In days gone by, you could offer a subscription to your newsletter and people would eagerly subscribe. Today, your opt-in gift needs to be compelling and of great interest to your audience. In the previous exercise you have the opportunity to create a compelling giveaway. Once you have that in place, add an opt-in form to your site, so people can subscribe to your list.

Here are the steps to getting your opt-in form onto your blog:

- ☐ Register for an email service, such as aWeber.com.
- ☐ Decide what downloadable gift you'll offer to your subscribers in exchange for their names and email addresses.
- ☐ Set up a "new list" in your email service.
- ☐ Under the list settings, you'll find a field that allows you to paste the URL to your hidden download page. Then when someone confirms their subscription, they'll automatically be taken to that page, as well as receive their thank you message.
- ☐ Create an opt-in form for this list
- ☐ Publish this form to your site by copying the code that is generated when you create your opt-in form.
- ☐ The most effective place to post an opt-in form is on your blog's sidebar.
- ☐ To add your form to the sidebar, in WordPress for example, go to the widgets page from your WordPress dashboard, and drag a "text" widget to the sidebar.
- ☐ You can then paste the code to your opt-in form into this text widget.
- ☐ Now it's time to test your opt-in form and delivery system to make sure that everything is lined up properly. Opt-in to the form to test this.

If any of the above sounds like a foreign language, don't worry! Take a deep breath and reach out to your email service's customer support or view their tutorials for step-by-step training.

# Create a Hidden Download Page

Today's action step is to create a hidden download page so you can easily deliver your opt-in gift. You need to have a way for your subscribers to receive their gift. Rather than giving them the link to the PDF file itself, it is more effective to post the download link on a hidden page on your blog.

A hidden page simply means that the name of the page does not show up in your site's navigation menu. Once someone subscribes to your email list, you can have your email system programed to automatically send out a thank you email, which includes a link to your hidden download page.

At the end of the day, journal your accomplishments in the section provided below. By prioritizing time to take action and reflect on your activity and results each day, you'll maximize the benefits you'll receive from this opportunity.

## What I Accomplished Today

# Action Steps

## Create a Hidden Download Page and Thank You Message

Creating a hidden thank you page is a great way to deliver your opt-in gift. That way, instead of simply getting access to the file, your subscribers will find themselves on your blog. Once they download their gift, they will likely explore your site, to find out more about you and your offerings.

Here's how to create a hidden download page and thank you message:

- ☐ Create a thank you page on your blog and upload your PDF gift.
- ☐ Include text on the page, thanking your subscribers and letting them know to click on the link to access their gift.
- ☐ Copy the URL to the PDF and hyperlink text on the page that says something like, "click here to access your gift."
- ☐ If you'd like, you can also invite subscribers to explore your site, or check out your book or program, for even more information on the topic.
- ☐ Publish this page as a hidden page (meaning the page title doesn't show up on your site's navigation menu.)
- ☐ Go to your email service and create a thank you follow up message that includes the URL to the hidden page where readers can access your gift.
- ☐ Set this to automatically go out (auto-responder) when someone subscribes.

Sample email template for your follow up email:

Hi [Add the short code, from your email service, for their first name]
Thank you for requesting your special gift of: _____
To claim your gift head over to: www._____
I look forward to getting to know you and welcome your questions.
To your success,
[Your Name]

Activity #12                    Date: _____

# Keep in Touch to Keep in Mind

Today's action step is to put a plan in place for keeping in touch with your email subscribers. The key to growing relationships with your subscribers is to provide them with valuable content on an ongoing basis.

When they opt-in to your list, they are expressing that they have an interest in what you have to offer. The key is to keep in touch on a regular basis by providing valuable and informative content.  If you email them "once in a blue moon" they may not remember who you are or why they subscribed to your list, which could cause them to unsubscribe.

At the end of the day, journal your accomplishments in the section provided below. By prioritizing time to take action and reflect on your activity and results each day, you'll maximize the benefits you'll receive from this opportunity.

## What I Accomplished Today

# Action Steps

## Keep in Touch to Keep in Mind

Think about the emails you receive. Which are the emails you scramble to open and which are the ones you dread or unsubscribe from. Typically people appreciate receiving helpful and informative email that is not too "salesy." While you can certainly recommend products or services or invite your readers to buy your book or register for one of your programs, the focus of your emails should be primarily on educating and connecting with your audience.

Here are some suggestions on how to gather content and generate ideas for emails you can send to your list:

- ☐ Make a list of major concerns, issues and topics relevant to your audience.

- ☐ Keep an ongoing list of ideas, as they come to mind.

- ☐ Create a survey that invites questions from your subscribers. You can do this with a free service such as Survey Monkey (www.surveymonkey.com).

- ☐ Browse relevant websites for topic ideas.

- ☐ If you read an article that you have a strong opinion on, write about it.

- ☐ Check the competition. See what competitors are talking about. Let this motivate a topic for an article, which you can email to your list.

What are some additional topics you could write about?

_____

_____

_____

_____

# Notes

# Step Four

## Increase Your Reach Through Guest Blogging

Activities
13-16

Guest blogging is where you write articles for other blogs in your niche. This is a wonderful way to gain credibility while receiving endorsements by blog owners, who attract your ideal readers.

You can write articles on topics related to your expertise, answer questions from readers, share top tips, and even share book excerpts.

Date: _____

# Discover the Power of Guest Blogging

Today's action step is to prepare to become a guest blogger. Guest blogging is where you are featured as a guest author on other peoples' blogs. The key, is to focus on getting featured on blogs that attract your niche audience. This is important as it will provide you with opportunities for getting in front of the exact readers who are interested in your topic.

Turn to the following page and identify what your audience is interested in, as they relate to your areas of expertise. By writing for blogs that attract your ideal readers, you will have the opportunity to share content with people who are likely to be interested in your book or program.

At the end of the day, journal your accomplishments in the section provided below. By prioritizing time to take action and reflect on your activity and results each day, you'll maximize the benefits you'll receive from this opportunity.

## What I Accomplished Today

# Action Steps

## Prepare to Become a Guest Blogger

As a guest blogger, it is essential that you locate and write articles for blogs that attract your ideal readers. Drawing from some of the exercises in Activity #2 on *Identifying Your Niche*, complete the worksheet below.

What are your areas of expertise?

- ○ _____
- ○ _____
- ○ _____
- ○ _____

What is your audience most interested in?

- ○ _____
- ○ _____
- ○ _____
- ○ _____

Compose a list of topics that you could write about, based on what your audiences is interested in, related to your areas of expertise. This will help you in the following activity, when you begin to locate blog related to these topics.

- ○ _____
- ○ _____
- ○ _____
- ○ _____

Activity #14                    Date: _____

# Locate and Reach Out to Potential Tour Hosts

Today's action step is to locate potential tour hosts for your virtual book tour. Begin by listing the blogs and blog owners you know or know of, who write on topics of interest to your audience.

When you visit those sites, look to see if they have other guest bloggers. If so, read through the blog posts of these guest bloggers. For those that you are inspired by, who write on topics that your ideal reader would be interested in, scroll down to the signature section of their post and click through to their blog. By doing this you'll be able to locate many more blogs in your niche.

At the end of the day, journal your accomplishments in the section provided below. By prioritizing time to take action and reflect on your activity and results each day, you'll maximize the benefits you'll receive from this opportunity.

## What I Accomplished Today

# Action Steps

## Locate and Line Up a Few Guest Blogging Tour Stops

Create a list of blogs, in your niche, that you'd like to write for.

- List the blogs of your colleagues and leaders in your field.
- Look for guest bloggers on those blogs. Add their blogs to your list.
- Go to www.BlogSearchEngine.org. Search for more blogs on your topic.
- Comment on blog posts and become an active reader.
- Reach out to the blog owners and invite them to be a tour host.

| Blog Owner's Name | Topic of Blog | Blog's Website Address |
|---|---|---|
| _____ | _____ | _____ |
| _____ | _____ | _____ |
| _____ | _____ | _____ |
| _____ | _____ | _____ |
| _____ | _____ | _____ |
| _____ | _____ | _____ |

**Sample Email:** Hi [name], I've been enjoying your blog and noticed that we share a common audience. In the coming months I will be participating in a virtual book tour for my book, [BOOK TITLE] and would love to feature your blog as a destination site during this tour.

The virtual book tour will provide you with exposure to audiences who are interested in your topic. Here is a link to my blog so you can see the quality of my writing. _____

I believe a guest blog post from me would benefit your readers and add to the great content you have on your blog.

You are of course under no obligation so please take a moment to reply and let me know whether or not you'd like me to reserve one of the featured tour stops for you. The dates of the tour are from: _____ to _____.

Thank you! With warmest regards, [Name]

# Set Up Your Virtual Tour Schedule Page

Today's action step is to set up your virtual tour schedule page. Having an easily accessible virtual book tour schedule page will increase your credibility as you'll be seen as an active guest blogger and one who associates with experts in your industry. A blog owner does not need to be a world-renowned expert in order to have expertise in their topic area.

Having a tour schedule page will also help you to keep organized and remind you of which tour stops are coming up and which sites to circle back to, to engage with readers and reply to comments.

At the end of the day, journal your accomplishments in the section provided below. By prioritizing time to take action and reflect on your activity and results each day, you'll maximize the benefits you'll receive from this opportunity.

## What I Accomplished Today

# Action Steps

## Set Up Your Virtual Book Tour Schedule Page

☐ Set up your virtual book tour schedule page and provide your audience with one handy location where they can access all the stops on your tour.

☐ List the date, host, and title of the blog post for each day of your tour.

☐ You can also send potential hosts to this page, once you have several of your tour stops listed. When a potential host sees that some of their friends and colleagues are participating, it will be easier for them to say "yes" to being a host for your tour.

☐ Wait until your post has been published to add the hyperlink to a tour destination. Take note that the URLs to your blog posts will not be valid until they day they are published. Until then the URL will lead to an error page.

☐ You may want to post a note at the top of your schedule page letting people know that each morning the URL to that day's tour stop will be posted.

☐ Once a date has passed, remove reference to the date. By doing this your content will remain current and evergreen that day, and into the future.

Here are the fields you'll want to include when adding a tour destination to your virtual tour schedule page:

Date:                    Host:                    Title of the Article You'll Be Sharing

_____            _____            _____

_____            _____            _____

_____            _____            _____

_____            _____            _____

# Develop a Blog Commenting Strategy

Today's action step is to develop a blog commenting strategy. Typically you're able to post comments below blog posts. This is an essential part of the blogging experience because you can interact with your readers by posting and responding to blog comments. You can also build relationships with readers and blog owners, which can lead to guest blogging opportunities.

Once your post is published to a blog, you'll want to be one of the first people to comment. In that initial comment you can thank your host for hosting you during your virtual book tour. You can also ask a question that engages readers.

At the end of the day, journal your accomplishments in the section provided below. By prioritizing time to take action and reflect on your activity and results each day, you'll maximize the benefits you'll receive from this opportunity.

## What I Accomplished Today

# Action Steps

## Develop a Blog Commenting Strategy

When blog owners see that you're knowledgeable in your topic area and that you're a giving person, because you're answering other people's questions and participating as a member of the community, you're more likely to be invited to be a guest blogger.

When leaving blog comments, you will be asked to fill out a form. These forms usually request your name, email address, and website address. The only person who will see your email address is the blog owner. By adding your website address, your name will show up as a hyperlink with your comment. When people click on this hyperlink, they will click through to your blog.

Another feature of a blog comment is the ability to pull in your photograph. This ads a personal touch and gives your comment more visibility.

To get your photograph to show up, you need to register your email address and upload a headshot photograph at: www.Gravatar.com Your gravatar is the photo that appears when you post blog comments.

Complete the following action steps and you'll see your photo show up when you post blog comments.

- ☐ Register for a Gravatar at www.Gravatar.com.

- ☐ Register with the email address you'll use when leaving comments.

- ☐ Upload a headshot photograph.

- ☐ Link your email to the photo, inside your Gravatar account.

- ☐ Post a comment to someone's blog.

- ☐ Watch your photo appear.

# Notes

# Step Five

## Create Content for Your Guest Blog Posts

Activities
17-20

Sharing content with your audience is the fun part and there are a wide variety of things you can share in your guest blog posts. You can talk about your author journey or the content of your book.

You can also take your readers on a journey as you share content that builds from one blog post to another, based on the chapter topics of your book for example.

# **Map Out Your Guest Blogging Content**

Today's action step is to outline or map out ideas for the content you'll share in your guest blog posts. As a guest blogger, you'll have opportunities to share your story and knowledge with your readers. You can be as creative as you'd like when composing the blog posts for your virtual book tour stops.

You may find it helpful to block out time, over a one to two week period, to create all your blog content. You can then check that off your list and focus on other aspects of your tour, such as interacting with hosts and new subscribers!

At the end of the day, journal your accomplishments in the section provided below. By prioritizing time to take action and reflect on your activity and results each day, you'll maximize the benefits you'll receive from this opportunity.

## What I Accomplished Today

# Action Steps

## Map Out Your Guest Blogging Content

Traditionally blog posts are written articles with accompanying images. The average size for a blog post is 450-600 words. When confirming with your tour hosts, ask them if they have a maximum and minimum word count requirement for blog posts. You can also ask if they accept original material that has been revised but previously published. Be sure to take careful notes on your master tour schedule page, in section one of this guide, so you can record any requirements your blog hosts have.

Here are examples of topics you could blog about:

☐ Talk about your author journey

☐ Share how you came to write your book

☐ Include book excerpts (if you have the rights to do so)

☐ Tell your characters' back stories or the story from a character's viewpoint

☐ Share lessons or top tips from your book

☐ Write about the message behind your book

☐ Share lessons or insights from your book

☐ Write how-to posts

What are some additional topics or ideas of things you could blog about?

○ _____

○ _____

○ _____

○ _____

○ _____

# Expanded Ideas for Blog Posts

_____

_____

_____

_____

_____

_____

_____

_____

_____

_____

_____

_____

_____

_____

_____

_____

_____

# Map Out Ideas for Your Blog Posts

In the first column brainstorm ideas for possible topics to blog about. In the second column, brainstorm ideas for possible titles for your posts.

## More Things to Blog About

☐ _____

_____

☐ _____

_____

☐ _____

_____

☐ _____

_____

☐ _____

_____

☐ _____

_____

☐ _____

_____

☐ _____

_____

## Possible Titles for My Posts

☐ _____

_____

☐ _____

_____

☐ _____

_____

☐ _____

_____

☐ _____

_____

☐ _____

_____

☐ _____

_____

☐ _____

_____

Activity #18 Date: _____

# Create a Signature Template for Your Blog Posts

Today's action step is to create a signature template for your blog posts. It is customary to include a 100-150 word signature section at the end of each of your posts. For maximum benefit, let readers know that they can receive a free gift (such as a checklist or top tips list) by going to your website. This will allow you to grow your email list. In your signature you can also include a short link to your book over on Amazon.

Turn to the following page and compose a signature section for your blog post. You can then copy it into a Word document for easy access.

At the end of the day, journal your accomplishments in the section provided below. By prioritizing time to take action and reflect on your activity and results each day, you'll maximize the benefits you'll receive from this opportunity.

## What I Accomplished Today

# Action Steps

## Create a Signature Template for Your Blog Posts

Your guest blog posts can serve as mini marketing machines for you. If you are writing for blogs that are of interest to your target audience, then they will likely be interested in your articles, your books and your services. One way to get people over to your blog is to have a well-crafted signature section at the bottom of each of your blog posts.

Your signature section is typically about 100 words in length and includes a compelling reason why people should come to your site. This "call to action" will encourage people to visit your blog where they will give you their name and email address in exchange for an opt-in giveaway.

Once you create your signature section, save it as a text or Word file on your computer. Then, each time you write a new blog post you can easily copy and paste your signature template at the bottom of the post.

**Template to Help you Compose a Signature Section for Your Posts**

(Name )_____ is the (author of or expert on): _____.

(One sentence that describes your experience) _____

_____

(One sentence that describes what "you do" or how you help people) _____

_____.

To learn more about (topic of post) claim your free gift of (description) at www.

Draw from the above and craft your signature template: _____

_____

_____

_____

Date: _____

# Get Your Posts to Your Hosts

Today's action step is to put systems in place for getting your blog posts to your hosts. It is a best practice to get your posts to your hosts a week or two before you'll be featured on their blog.

Blog posts can be set to automatically publish on a specific date and time. Encourage your hosts to publish your posts the night before the date you are scheduled to travel to their blog. That way you can begin promoting first thing the morning you are scheduled to travel to their blog.

At the end of the day, journal your accomplishments in the section provided below. By prioritizing time to take action and reflect on your activity and results each day, you'll maximize the benefits you'll receive from this opportunity.

## What I Accomplished Today

# Action Steps

## Get Your Posts to Your Hosts

Here is a checklist to help you streamline your blog posts.

- ☐ Get your posts to your hosts ahead of time, ideally one to two weeks before your tour date to their site.

- ☐ When you send a post to a host, request that they publish it and send you the URL. Some will publish it to go "live" immediately while others will wait until your scheduled tour date.

- ☐ Until a post goes live, the URL will appear as an error page. That is normal.

- ☐ Write your hosts the day before you tour to their blog to thank them and let them know you'll be promoting their blog and posting a comment as soon as the post goes live on their blog.

**Sample Email to Send to Your Hosts**

Hi [Name], thank you for hosting me during my virtual book tour. You'll find my blog post attached.

Could you please post it to your blog and send me the URL to where it will appear live on [Day and Date – Time Zone]. That way it will be available for me to begin promoting, first thing that morning. If you'd prefer to schedule it to go live now, that's fine too.

Please send me the URL to where it will appear or please confirm the date that you have it in your calendar to get that to me.

Thanks again! I look forward to sharing your blog as a destination on this virtual book tour. With much appreciation, [Your Name]

Activity #20                     Date: _____

# Compose Mini Posts for Your Tour Stops

Today's action step is to create mini posts for your blog, announcing each of your tour stops. Mini posts are 200-300 word teaser posts on your blog, letting readers know where you'll be going each day of your tour. They can be engaging and get people excited about what you'll be writing or speaking about.

Mini posts provide you with a way to drive web traffic from the social networks to your blog and from your blog to your tour stops. This type of activity can help with your blog's search engine rankings.

At the end of the day, journal your accomplishments in the section provided below. By prioritizing time to take action and reflect on your activity and results each day, you'll maximize the benefits you'll receive from this opportunity.

## What I Accomplished Today

# Action Steps

## Compose Mini Posts for Your Tour Stops

As part of your virtual book tour, you can also travel to your own blog. Here's an exercise that will help to prepare you for writing mini posts throughout your virtual book tour.

- ☐ Write a blog post for your own blog. It could be about your upcoming virtual book tour, about your book, or about something to do with your area of expertise.

- ☐ Publish the post to your blog and include your signature template at the end of your post.

- ☐ Next, create a mini post that includes a brief description of your full blog post.

- ☐ Leave readers at a cliff-hanger and invite them to click on a link to read the full article.

Use the space below to write a rough draft of a mini post for your blog.

_____

_____

_____

_____

_____

_____

# Notes

# Step Six

## *Harness the Power of Online Author Interviews*

**Activities 21-24**

Author interviews provide you with a powerful way to connect with your audience and leaders in your field. When people hear your voice, they will connect with you at a deeper level.

Participating in author interviews also increases your credibility as you'll get endorsed by your interview hosts!

Date: _____

# Discover the Power of Author Interviews

Today's action step is to explore the possibilities that online interviews offer. They can provide you with wonderful exposure and opportunities to connect with your listeners. This can expand your online presence and your book sales.

By being a guest speaker, you'll be able to reach more readers and increase your visibility. Online interviews are fun and easy to record, and are easily accessible to your audience. By being a guest on interviews, you don't have to worry about any technology, as your host takes care of that from their end.

At the end of the day, journal your accomplishments in the section provided below. By prioritizing time to take action and reflect on your activity and results each day, you'll maximize the benefits you'll receive from this opportunity.

## What I Accomplished Today

# Action Steps

## Discover the Power of Author Interviews

○ Author interviews provide a wonderful platform for promoting your book and brand while getting introduced to new audiences.

○ Providing ways for your audience to connect with you and hear the message of your book will increase your book sales.

○ By being a guest speaker on podcasts, teleseminars, and Internet radio shows, you'll be able to reach more readers and increase your credibility.

○ By being a guest speaker, you are being endorsed by your hosts and giving listeners the opportunity to get to know you.

○ Participating in author interviews—or talking about your book over the air waves—is a powerful way for your audience to hear your voice and connect with you.

○ Author interviews provide you with a way to share your brilliance and your experience with people interested in your topic area.

○ In addition to your live interviews, the audio recordings can be made available for people to listen to at their convenience.

What excites you most about participating in online interviews?

○ _____

○ _____

○ _____

In what ways will your audience benefit by hearing about your book?

○ _____

○ _____

○ _____

# Activity #22

## Prepare Your Speaker Introduction

Today's action step is to prepare your speaker bio introduction. This is what your host will read when they introduce you at the beginning of the call. Your speaker bio is a brief statement which highlights your experience and shines the spotlight on your credibility.

This will give your listeners a brief but powerful glimpse at who you are and what you do. In addition to your credentials and accomplishments, share a sentence or two about how you help the audience you serve.

At the end of the day, journal your accomplishments in the section provided below. By prioritizing time to take action and reflect on your activity and results each day, you'll maximize the benefits you'll receive from this opportunity.

### What I Accomplished Today

# Craft Your Speaker Bio

Use the following template to compose your speaker bio. Strive to keep your bio to 100-125 words, unless your host indicates otherwise. This way you'll focus on what's essential and will retain the attention of your listeners.

(Name )_____ of (URL) www._____

is the (author of or expert on): _____.

(One sentence that describe your experience) _____

_____

(One sentence that describes what "you do" or how you help people) _____

_____.

Today (name) will be speaking to us about: _____.

Draw from the above outline to compose your speaker bio: _____

_____

_____

_____

Hot Tip: Typically, at the end of an interview, the host will ask you to let people know the best way to get in touch with you. Rather than giving your listeners multiple options, give them one URL so they take action.

The most effective option is to let them know, with your host's permission, that you have a special gift for them, which they can receive by going to your blog. Provide them with the URL to where they go to register their name and email address in exchange for your gift. This will get them onto your email list.

You'll then have the opportunity to build ongoing relationships with your new subscribers.

# Activity #23

Date: _____

## Participate in Practice Interviews

Today's action step is to prepare to participate in practice interviews. Begin by preparing your interview questions. While some hosts have questions they work from, it is a common practice to provide a list of proposed questions to your interview hosts. By providing a list of suggested questions, you'll be able to speak on topics that feature your strengths, on a topic you are familiar with.

Many guest speakers select questions based on their book, their topic, or their signature speech, as this draws on their experience and areas of expertise. Your host can use these as the foundation of your interview.

At the end of the day, journal your accomplishments in the section provided below. By prioritizing time to take action and reflect on your activity and results each day, you'll maximize the benefits you'll receive from this opportunity.

### What I Accomplished Today

# Compose a List of Interview Questions

Draw from the suggestions below to compose a list of 8-12 questions.

## For All Authors

- ○ Tell us a bit about your success journey.
- ○ How did you come up with the idea for your book?
- ○ Can you please share a brief synopsis of your book?
- ○ Who is your ideal reader?
- ○ What is the best way for people to connect with you?
- ○ What thoughts would you like to leave our listeners with?

## For Nonfiction Authors

- ○ How did you get interested in this topic area?
- ○ Could you please share 3 top tips from your book?
- ○ What is one thing our listeners can do, in the next 24 hours, to take action on what they learned during this interview?

## For Fiction Authors

- ○ What do you enjoy most about your genre?
- ○ Are your characters in your book based on people in your life?
- ○ Who is your favorite character and why?

Compose additional questions below.

- ○ _____
- ○ _____
- ○ _____

Open up a Word document and compose your master list of interview questions. Save these to a folder on your hard drive.

Date: _____

# Locate and Schedule Interview Hosts

Today's action step is to locate and schedule interview hosts. The easiest way to get started with online speaking is to interview and get interviewed by people you already know, who attract members of your target audience. Once the interview has concluded, be sure to thank your hosts and ask them for referrals to others who interview, in your niche.

Have fun with these interviews and treat them as enjoyable conversations with friends. Share your brilliance and your passion for your topic and allow your listeners to get a sense of who you are and what's important to you.

At the end of the day, journal your accomplishments in the section provided below. By prioritizing time to take action and reflect on your activity and results each day, you'll maximize the benefits you'll receive from this opportunity.

## What I Accomplished Today

# Action Steps

## Locate Online Speaking Opportunities

Compose a list of potential interview hosts and reach out to line up interviews.

☐ Turn back to activity #19 and draw from the email template to blog hosts when composing an email template for potential interview hosts.

| Name of Host | Name of Show or Podcast | Website Address |
|---|---|---|
| _____ | _____ | _____ |
| _____ | _____ | _____ |
| _____ | _____ | _____ |
| _____ | _____ | _____ |
| _____ | _____ | _____ |
| _____ | _____ | _____ |

To locate additional online speaking opportunities, go to iTunes and BlogTalkRadio.com and search for hosts and shows on your topic area.

| Name of Host | Name of Show or Podcast | Website Address |
|---|---|---|
| _____ | _____ | _____ |
| _____ | _____ | _____ |
| _____ | _____ | _____ |
| _____ | _____ | _____ |
| _____ | _____ | _____ |

# Notes

# Step Seven

## *Promote Your Virtual Book Tour*

Activities
25-28

Now that you have an understanding and some practical application of putting a virtual book tour together, it's time to share it with the world.

Promoting your virtual tour can be a lot of fun and it's a wonderful way to connect with your hosts and with members of your niche audience.

# Activity #25

## Create Graphics for Your Virtual Book Tour

Today's action step is to create graphics to generate interest in your virtual book tour. On the social networks, one way to stand out from the crowd is to upload an image along with your written post.

There are many ways to create online graphics. Canva.com provides one of the easiest online graphic sites on the Internet. The simplest type of graphic to create is one where you use a visually engaging background and superimpose text on top of it. Canva provides you with a wide variety of templates and designs that you can use to easily create graphics.

At the end of the day, journal your accomplishments in the section provided below. By prioritizing time to take action and reflect on your activity and results each day, you'll maximize the benefits you'll receive from this opportunity.

## What I Accomplished Today

# Action Steps

## Create Graphics for Each Day of Your Virtual Book Tour

Gather ideas for the graphics you'd like to create for your virtual book tour. You can add text to an image and use that image to promote your tour.

Inspiring or Thought Provoking Quotes from Your Book

○ _____

_____

○ _____

_____

○ _____

_____

Host Name and Blog or Interview Topic for Each Day of Your Tour

○ _____

○ _____

○ _____

○ _____

○ _____

○ _____

○ _____

○ _____

○ _____

## **Promote Your Tour to the Social Networks**

Today's action step is to promote your virtual book tour via the social networks. This can be a lot of fun and create wonderful engagement with your audience. In a previous activity you learned how to create a Facebook page for your virtual book tour. That is one of the places to post links to your tour stops.

Throughout your tour, create a habit of posting announcements as to where you will be "traveling" to each day of your tour. Schedule this time in your calendar as this consistency will allow you to build momentum.

At the end of the day, journal your accomplishments in the section provided below. By prioritizing time to take action and reflect on your activity and results each day, you'll maximize the benefits you'll receive from this opportunity.

### What I Accomplished Today

# Action Steps

## Promote Your Virtual Book Tour via the Social Networks

During your book tour, you'll want to find ways to create buzz. The most effective way to do this is to post announcements on social networks and ask your followers to help spread the word. Compose a list of things you can post to the social networks. Here are is an example to draw from.

It's day #_____ of the virtual book tour for [name of book] _____.
Today I'm traveling to the [blog or podcast] _____ of [host's name] _____ where I'll be sharing _____. Join us at: www.

_____

_____

_____


_____

_____

_____


_____

_____

_____


_____

_____

_____

## **Automate Social Media Posts with Hootsuite**

Today's action step is to automate your social media posts with HootSuite Hootsuite.com is an online service that allows you to simplify and streamline your social media posts and post to several social networks at the same time.

HootSuite also makes it easy for you to locate relevant content based on search criteria, such as hashtags, Twitter groups, keywords, and more. Visit Hootsuite's "product support" tab to view tutorials. Streamlining your social media activities will allow you to become more active and productive.

At the end of the day, journal your accomplishments in the section provided below. By prioritizing time to take action and reflect on your activity and results each day, you'll maximize the benefits you'll receive from this opportunity.

### What I Accomplished Today

# Compose Tweets to Schedule in Hootsuite

Tweet an Inspiring Quote: _____

_____

_____


Tweet About Your Latest Blog Post: _____

_____

_____


Tweet About Your Most Recent Interview: _____

_____

_____


Tweet About _____: _____

_____

_____


Tweet About _____: _____

_____

_____

Activity #28                  Date: _____

# Create a Buzz with Book Reviews

Today's action step is to ask readers to post reviews for your book on Amazon. This will create a buzz and boost your book sales, as this type of social proof demonstrates that your book is popular and people like it. You can then post those reviews on a "Reviews" page on your blog.

Begin by promoting your book to your email subscribers and inviting them to post a review to Amazon. These are followers of your work and many of them will likely be interested in purchasing and reviewing your book. Seeing reviews on Amazon will encourage other readers to post their reviews.

At the end of the day, journal your accomplishments in the section provided below. By prioritizing time to take action and reflect on your activity and results each day, you'll maximize the benefits you'll receive from this opportunity.

## What I Accomplished Today

# Action Steps

## Create a Buzz with Book Reviews

Compose a brief message that introduces your email subscribers to your book. Include an invitation to post a review on Amazon and thank them for their support. You could also let them know that as part of your book tour, you will be inviting them to a special online book talk where they'll have a chance to "Ask the Author" questions.

Prepare a message that you can send your email subscribers. Let them know that a book review can be a brief paragraph.

_____

_____

_____

_____

_____

_____

_____

Compose a list of people you know, who support and believe in your work, and ask them for a book review. In some cases you may want to mail them a signed copy of your book.

○ _____

○ _____

○ _____

○ _____

○ _____

○ _____

# Notes

# Step Eight
## Take Your Book on the Virtual Tour Road

Activities 29-30

Now that you have all of the pieces of the jigsaw puzzle in place or as you continue to put all of the jigsaw puzzle pieces in place, make it a priority to keep your momentum going.

Time ticks by, regardless of what we do or do not do. With that in mind, schedule time in your calendar for when you want to conduct your tour, as well as for when you'll take ongoing action to organize, manage, and market your tour.

Activity #29                    Date: _____

# Complete Your Virtual Book Tour Checklist

Today's action step is to review the tasks presented up until this point and take stock of what you've completed and what still needs to be put in place.

If you wait for everything to be perfect, you may never roll out your tour. Instead, take imperfect action and enjoy sharing your book and your message, connecting with your audience and selling more books! A virtual book tour is a work in progress. Decide on your tour dates and then map out a plan for putting things in place to prepare for your tour. Many of the marketing and promotion tasks can take place during your virtual tour.

At the end of the day, journal your accomplishments in the section provided below. By prioritizing time to take action and reflect on your activity and results each day, you'll maximize the benefits you'll receive from this opportunity.

## What I Accomplished Today

# Action Steps

## Reflections and Checklist for Your Virtual Book Tour

While there are many moving parts to a virtual tour, **you do not** have to have them all in place to begin planning, conducting, or marketing your tour. Your virtual book tour efforts can be a work in progress, that come together as you move along. On the following pages you'll find a list of the key virtual book tour activities. Plug them into your calendar & check them off as you complete them.

What are the dates for your virtual book tour? _____

What excites you most about conducting a virtual book tour for your book?

_____

_____

_____

What would it mean for you to get your book and your message in front of a whole lot more readers?

_____

_____

_____

What challenges are you experiencing at this time?

○ _____

○ _____

○ _____

What can you do to overcome these challenges in order to get your virtual book tour moving forward?

○ _____

○ _____

○ _____

# Checklist for Your Virtual Book Tour

## Step 1: Set the Stage for Your Virtual Book Tour

- ☐ Get clear on your virtual tour goals.
- ☐ Identify your niche/target audience.
- ☐ Decide on the dates for your tour.
- ☐ Reach out and line up a few tour hosts.

## Step 2: Develop Your Author Platform

- ☐ Get your blog ready for company.
- ☐ Enhance your Amazon Author page.
- ☐ Streamline your social media profiles.
- ☐ Set up your Facebook page.

## Step 3: Build Ongoing Relationships with Your Readers

- ☐ Create a downloadable subscriber opt-in gift.
- ☐ Add an opt-in form on your blog.
- ☐ Create a hidden download page.
- ☐ Keep in touch to keep in mind.

## Step 4: Increase Your Reach Through Guest Blogging

- ☐ Discover the power of guest blogging.
- ☐ Locate and reach out to potential tour hosts.
- ☐ Set up your virtual book tour schedule page.
- ☐ Develop a blog commenting strategy.

# Checklist for Your Virtual Book Tour

## Step 5: Create Content for Your Guest Blog Posts

- ☐ Map out your guest blogging content.
- ☐ Create a signature template for your posts.
- ☐ Get your posts to your hosts.
- ☐ Compose mini posts for your tour stops.

## Step 6: Harness the Power of Online Author Interviews

- ☐ Discover the power of author interviews.
- ☐ Prepare your speaker introduction.
- ☐ Participate in practice interviews
- ☐ Locate and schedule interview hosts.

## Step 7: Promote Your Virtual Book Tour

- ☐ Create graphics for your virtual book tour.
- ☐ Promote your tour to the social networks.
- ☐ Automate social media posts with Hootsuite.
- ☐ Create a buzz with book reviews.

## Step 8: Take Your Book on the Virtual Tour Road

- ☐ Complete your virtual tour checklist.
- ☐ Celebrate and keep the momentum going.

_____

_____

_____

_____

_____

Activity #30                    Date: _____

## Celebrate and Keep the Momentum Going

Today's action step is to celebrate your accomplishments and put a plan in place to keep your momentum going. Open up your calendar and schedule times to develop and conduct your virtual book tour.

Congratulations, you made it! But, the journey doesn't end here. You'll want to put a plan in place to keep your momentum going. Wherever you are on the spectrum, from brainstorming ideas to conducting your virtual book tour, you are only a decision away from taking your book tour on the virtual road.

At the end of the day, journal your accomplishments in the section provided below. By prioritizing time to take action and reflect on your activity and results each day, you'll maximize the benefits you'll receive from this opportunity.

### What I Accomplished Today

# Action Steps

## Time to Celebrate and Keep the Momentum Going

Wherever you are on this virtual book tour journey, it's time to celebrate your accomplishments! Wherever you are, in the process of planning or conducting your tour, you are in the perfect place! The key is to keep the momentum going. Complete this worksheet and schedule time to keep the ball rolling forward.

Where I am at in regards to preparing and conducting my tour:

○ _____

○ _____

○ _____

What I've accomplished so far:

_____   _____

_____   _____

_____   _____

What I will do to celebrate my accomplishments:

○ _____

○ _____

○ _____

What my next steps are:

○ _____

○ _____

○ _____

# Virtual Book Tour Journal

Date: _____

_____

_____

_____

_____

_____

_____

Date: _____

_____

_____

_____

_____

_____

_____

Date: _____

_____

_____

_____

_____

_____

Date: _____

_____

_____

_____

_____

_____

# Virtual Book Tour Journal

Date: _____

_____

_____

_____

_____

_____

_____

Date: _____

_____

_____

_____

_____

_____

_____

Date: _____

_____

_____

_____

_____

_____

_____

Date: _____

_____

_____

_____

_____

_____

_____

# Virtual Book Tour Journal

Date: _____

_____

_____

_____

_____

_____

_____

Date: _____

_____

_____

_____

_____

_____

_____

Date: _____

_____

_____

_____

_____

_____

_____

Date: _____

_____

_____

_____

_____

_____

_____

# Virtual Book Tour Journal

Date: _____

_____

_____

_____

_____

_____

_____

Date: _____

_____

_____

_____

_____

_____

_____

Date: _____

_____

_____

_____

_____

_____

_____

Date: _____

_____

_____

_____

_____

_____

_____

# Virtual Book Tour Journal

Date: _____

_____

_____

_____

_____

_____

_____

Date: _____

_____

_____

_____

_____

_____

_____

Date: _____

_____

_____

_____

_____

_____

_____

Date: _____

_____

_____

_____

_____

_____

_____

# Virtual Book Tour Journal

Date: _____

_____

_____

_____

_____

_____

_____

Date: _____

_____

_____

_____

_____

_____

_____

Date: _____

_____

_____

_____

_____

_____

_____

Date: _____

_____

_____

_____

_____

_____

_____

# Virtual Book Tour Journal

Date: _____          Date: _____

_____                _____

_____                _____

_____                _____

_____                _____

_____                _____

_____                _____

Date: _____          Date: _____

_____                _____

_____                _____

_____                _____

_____                _____

_____                _____

# Virtual Book Tour Journal

Date: _____

_____

_____

_____

_____

_____

_____

_____

Date: _____

_____

_____

_____

_____

_____

_____

_____

Date: _____

_____

_____

_____

_____

_____

_____

_____

Date: _____

_____

_____

_____

_____

_____

_____

_____

# About D'vorah

D'vorah Lansky, M.Ed., is the bestselling author of several books including; *Book Marketing Made Easy: Simple Strategies for Selling Your Nonfiction Book* Online and the *Productivity Action Guide for Authors: 90 Days to a More Productive You.* She's also the founder and producer of the Annual Book Marketing Conference Online.

Through her coaching and training programs, D'vorah has taught thousands of authors how to effectively and affordably market their books online.

# Books by D'vorah

Check out all of D'vorah's books at: www.BooksByDvorah.com

Her flagship book is *Book Marketing Made Easy: Simple Strategies for Selling Your Nonfiction Book Online.* Discover the secrets that successful authors use to market their books online.

In *Book Marketing Made Easy* you will learn how to: increase your credibility and be seen as an expert in your field, sell more books to people who will benefit from your message, create multiple sources of income with the content of your book, harness the power of multimedia marketing to reach more readers, and use social media to increase your influence and expand your market.

Available on Amazon or a bookstore near you!
ISBN: 978-0965197595

# Action Guides for Authors

These take-action workbooks and journals are designed to help you track your activities & results so you can reach more readers & sell more books.

**ActionGuidesForAuthors.com**

## The Busy Author's Journal Series

The Busy Author's Journal series provides you with 30-day journals designed to help you monitor and track your daily activities and your results. By doing something, even something small each day, you will make a huge splash as you reach more readers, sell more books, and help more people.

## The 30-Day Challenge for Authors Series

In the 30-Day Challenge for Authors series, you have access to step-by-step training and action steps to help you accomplish the tasks laid out in each guide. Over the course of 30 days, you'll take bite-sized action steps as you fit the pieces of the jigsaw puzzle in place.

**Available on Amazon at BooksByDvorah.com**

www.ingramcontent.com/pod-product-compliance
Lightning Source LLC
Chambersburg PA
CBHW082110070326
40689CB00052B/4491